ELECTRA

Sophocles'

ELECTRA

Adapted by
FRANK McGUINNESS

ISBN: 0-7394-0365-6

Manufactured in the U.S.A.

A NOTE FROM THE DIRECTOR

During the war in Bosnia, a friend brought me a short amateur documentary film from Sarajevo. It was mainly an account of the lives of a group of children, all of whom had suffered the loss of someone close to them—a father, a mother, a brother, a sister—as a result of the war.

Of the many shocks in this film, one image struck with unforgettable force. It was a young girl whose brother had been killed in a mortar attack on his school. She had been unable, or simply refused, to speak since his death. Occasionally her face would crease with unbearable sadness, but otherwise there were almost no clues as to the huge turmoil and pain moving inside her.

Towards the end of the film she is seen coming out of her house on a snowy day with a bar of chocolate in her hand. She makes her way along the path to the makeshift cemetery where her brother lies. Brushing the snow from his grave, she carefully places the chocolate there. Then from her overcoat pocket, she takes one of his toy racing cars to set it down beside him.

And all the time she is whispering to him.

It is, of course, the kind of image that almost defeats speech and reason. But anyone would wonder what the wounds this young girl harbors in her heart will become over time and as she becomes a woman. What flowers will grow from the seeds?

When Sophocles wrote *Electra* over 2,000 years ago, it was precisely to attempt to find both speech and reason to confront the most fundamental moral struggles in the heart of civilization itself. And the force of his play is in the fact that the great issues of human and social experience, before which we might otherwise be left speechless and alone, are uttered as words *for the very first time*. And the arguments of the play are so fundamental, and so originally human, that they literally echo down through history, like a kind of blueprint against which all the repetitions of experience in our world can be measured. And confronted.

The apparently inescapable cycle of violence set off by inter-family or civil war, and the distortions inflicted upon the personality and a whole society by hatred—these are of course issues of our own century which, though it may just about have been bettered for barbarism by other eras, is probably so far uniquely suicidal.

Electra's uncompromising insistence on vengeance and the imperative of honoring the innocent dead divides her savagely from her sister Chrysothemis' humane spirit of tolerance. Their argument is a moral struggle that resonates now from the Balkans to the streets of Omagh. Above all, it asks if justice devoid of forgiveness may really be considered 'just' at all. And in the anguished image of a family divided from itself, the play's moral landscape also lays before us the less 'rational' complexities and ambiguities that lie deep within the psyche and drive our actions—daughters' relationships to their fathers, sons' to their mothers, mothers' to their daughters and their sons—these are also power for the first time, to be checked against our own experience.

In practice, Sophocles accompanies every compelling argument in the play with a breathtaking silence from others on the stage—and, you could argue, from heaven itself. This is not a solemn or enigmatic silence (and certainly not something to do with 'classical style'). It has what authentic silence in modern theatre has—a moral force. By absenting himself—and the gods—from judgment, Sophocles leaves us with the moral *processes* that confront us, not the moral 'solutions'. That is no evasion, of course, it is probably the absolute condition of useful wisdom—and responsibility.

All this distilled down to a single place, on a single day, gives the play its enormously energetic compression, vast scale, and sensational beauty—it is an austere 'sonata,' but lyrically miraculous nonetheless. Maybe, above all, it is an overcoming of an inconsolable silence in the face of sudden death. And to that extent makes us fractionally less alone.

Electra is not an obscure classic, a strange story of a distant time and place and people. It is, in every sense, our story. And perhaps we can say that a great play earns our enduring love not only because it is a courageous account of its own times, but also because it is a prophecy. And a prophecy that has to be learned time and time again. Which is what connects Electra, weeping over Orestes' ashes, to a place two millennia later and just a few hundred miles from where the play was first performed, and a young girl whispering to her dead brother in the snow.

David Leveaux

ELECTRA was produced by Eric Krebs, Randall L. Wreghitt, Anita Waxman, Elizabeth Peck Williams, and Lawrence Horowitz in association with the McCarter Theatre/Donmar Warehouse and Duncan C. Weldon Productions, at the Ethel Barrymore Theatre in New York City, opening on December 3, 1998. The cast was as follows:

Servant to Orestes	Stephen Spinella
Orestes	Michael Cumpsty
Pylades	Ivan Stamenov
Electra	Zoë Wanamaker
Chorus	Mirjana Jokovic
Chorus of Mycenae	Pat Carroll
Chorus	Myra Lucretia Taylor
Chrysothemis	Marin Hinkle
Clytemnestra	Claire Bloom
Aegisthus	Daniel Oreskes
Director	David Leveaux
Set and Costume Design	Johan Engels
Lighting Design	Paul Pyant
Sound Design	T. Richard Fitzgerald

This adaptation was originally produced in the United States by McCarter Theatre, Princeton, NJ, Emily Mann, Artistic Director/Jeffrey Woodward, Managing Director, on September 18, 1998.

This new version of ELECTRA by Frank McGuinness was commissioned by the Donmar Warehouse with first performances at the Chichester Festival Theatre on September 11, 1997 and at the Donmar Warehouse Theatre on October 21, 1997.

BACKGROUND TO THE STORY

Agamemnon, King of Mycenae and father to Electra and Orestes, sacrificed their sister Iphigenia to appease the gods as he led the Greek fleet to war with Troy. During his absence, his wife, Clytemnestra, Electra's mother, took Aegisthus as a lover. On Agamemnon's victorious return from Troy, they assassinated him. The infant Orestes was snatched to safety by his sister and sent away into hiding. Electra, haunted with love for her dead father, awaits the return of Orestes and retribution.

For Ann Bourke

An old Servant enters with Orestes and Pylades.

Servant

Son of Agamemnon,
This is your father's land, the ancient city of Argos.
How long have you waited for this happy sight?
Observe it.
From here your father led the Greeks to Troy.
Here that poor demented creature, Io, wandered.
There's the market place called after Apollo.
Hera's shrine, so famous, lies to your left.
This is Mycenae,
It is beneath our feet, rich Mycenae,
Blood-red Mycenae, the murderous home of Pelops'
sons.
I carried you once from this place.
Your sister snatched you from your father's corpse.
And I received you into my hands
To rear you till you were man enough
To revenge yourself against your father's murder.
That time is now, Orestes,
The hour is now,
Do it now. Decide what to do.
The day is breaking to the birds' voices.
The stars have shrunk,
The night is nothing.
Before a soul stirs out of their sleep,
Do not pause.
Decide what to do. Do it now.

Orestes

Best of men,
Your loyalty shines.

A great steed may be on his last legs
But he still relishes the scent of danger.
That's the spirit in you.
Listen to me, I will tell you all,
And if I miss the mark tell me.
When I went to Delphi to ask Apollo,
How do I revenge my father's murder?
The oracle told me this.
I must use my own cunning to do the deed.
And not trust arms nor men.
In the light of that oracle.
When you get a chance, go into the house,
Find out everything they're up to.
And bring it back to me!
No one will suspect you.
Your white hair, your tired face have transformed
you.
Tell them some story.
Say you are a foreigner,
You've come from Phocis, sent by Phanoteus,
He's one of their bosom pals,
And then, on your oath, you must swear—
Orestes is dead!
There was an accident—he fell from his chariot
As he raced in the games at Delphi.
Spin them that yarn.
We'll go first to my father's tomb, and honour it,
We'll spill wine and leave a lock of hair,
As Apollo ordered us to do.
We'll carry back that bronze urn, hidden in the
bushes,
And entertain them with the deception
That I am burnt to ashes.

Will that bring bad luck?
So what if the word is I am dead,
When the truth is I am safe and sound,
Ready to earn my fame.
Words used to your advantage can't bring bad.
I've heard of heroes in the past,
They were presumed dead and when they rose again,
The honour given to them was all the greater.
The rumour of my sad story will do just that.
I will blaze like a meteor through my enemies.
But grant me good luck, you, my home.
My father's house,
My father's land.
My father's gods.
For those same gods have hastened me here
To scrub you clean of stain.
Don't let me be dishonoured,
Don't send me from this land.
Let me prosper,
Let me put this house back on its feet.
I have said enough.
Old man, do what you have to do.
We will do the same.
The time's come, and no man cheats time.

(*Electra howls from within*)

Servant

Some servant woman is crying inside.

Orestes

Electra—could it be her weeping?
Could we stay and hear what breaks her heart?

Servant

We could not.
You do what Apollo demands, he is a god.
He knows what we should do.
Pour wine on your father's grave.
Agamemnon. His tomb.
He will help us.
And we'll succeed. We will succeed.

(*They exit. Electra enters from the palace, chanting*)

Electra

Divine light,
Sweet air,
Again hear
My pain.
Divine light,
Sweet air,
Again hear
My pain.
Have you not witnessed when morning breaks
My heart break, my heart break?
When night falls, I do not feast
In this house of ghosts.
I lie alone.
My father's dead.
He did not die in war.
He does not lie on a foreign shore.
Here, at home,
My mother's hands turned red
With his blood. Adulteress,
Adulterer, she and Aegisthus,
Split him open with an axe.

The tree fell,
And father, I am left to dwell
Alone in your house, my back
Against the wall,
Weeping for my father dead,
Mourning my dead father.
But I swear, while my eyes see
The sun or stars in the sky,
I will never cease to cry out
My pain and my complaint.
I will be like the poor nightingale
Who killed her young,
Then sorrow raped her heart.
That is the song I will spill
Through this house where blood was spilt.
I call upon Persephone,
I call upon the dead,
I call upon the Furies,
Revenge my father's blood-stained marriage
  bed,
Revenge my father,
Send me back my brother,
I can no longer stomach the size of my sorrow.

(*The Chorus enters*)

Chorus

Electra, child, you're wasting away with grief.
Because your mother's heartless, you're left to
  mourn the cruel fate of your father.
She betrayed him, and her lover knifed him.
A dirty death's in store for sinners of that nature.
May the gods forgive me saying it.

Electra

You're good people. You've come to comfort me.
I do know you have kind hearts.
But you should know I have a job to do,
And that is to weep sore tears over my dead father.
You pay kindness back with kindness, you're my friends,
So I beg you, leave me be, leave me.

Chorus

Your father is dead.
You can't cry him back from his grave.
Your prayers can't raise him up again.
You will die from all this grieving.
Will you not rest from it, when it will bring you no remedy?
It is pointless—why do you persist?

Electra

It's a cruel child that forgets a father's cruel end.
I'd sooner turn to stone and my tears into rivers.

Chorus

You're not alone in your sorrow—others share your burden.
Your sisters Iphianassa and Chrysothemis.
They feel their affliction too. Think of them.
Think of your brother in his sorrow,
A young man far from his home.
Heaven send him here to us soon, Orestes;
He'll make Mycenae his own, he'll take his father's throne.

Electra

I've waited for him long years,
Crying barren spinsters' tears.
I'm drenched lamenting my fate.
The many wrongs we've suffered.
He knows them all—not a word.
I hear he dreams he'll come home.
It's buried deep in his bones.
Aye, let him dream, we must wait.

Chorus

Keep your strength, girl, have strength.
God is still great in his heaven, and he sees
everything.
Offer up to him what is eating you inside.
Don't go on fire with hatred.
Remember this—time's a gentle god, he heals.
Agamemnon's son may wander the plains of Crisa,
But he will not forget his father,
And the God of Death will not forget either.

Electra

The best days of my life are finished.
I have neither hope nor strength.
I'm a childless woman who is melting away.
I have no man to protect me.
I live like a slave in my father's house.
I dress like a beggar—eat what's thrown me.

Chorus

A terrible cry greeted your father home,
And he gave a terrible cry in return.
The blow of the axe cut him in two.

They were as cunning as they were passionate,
And they did the deed. Where did it spring from?
This filthy act—was it God or man?

Electra

That cursed day, that sorest night,
At the feast to welcome him home
They cut my father like meat.
They laid their hands upon him.
They took his life, took my life.
Great God in heaven, hear me.
Make them suffer, make them weep.
May their power turn to nothing.
May they die and turn to nothing.

Chorus

Hold your tongue.
Has it never dawned on you how much you make
your own misery?
You pile on your agony.
You're a feeble woman fighting mighty enemies.

Electra

I have harmed myself by the harm done to me.
I know the hardness of my heart.
But as long as there is breath left in my body,
I will not change direction no matter how harmful.
Dear sisters if you admit the truth,
What word of comfort could console me?
There is no end to my lamenting.
There never will be an end to my sorrow.

Chorus

Well don't add sorrow on to sorrow.
I'm speaking as a friend, a mother you can trust.

Electra

What limit is there to what torments me?
Tell me, is it an honour to forget the dead?
Is it in the nature of the living to do that?
If there are such people, may they scorn me.
And if I possess anything good that I value,
May I lose it if I stop this mourning,
If I dishonour—if I forget my father.
If a dead man is to turn to dirt and nothing,
And those who did it do not pay the wages of their sin,
If they themselves are not murdered in return,
Then the gods are dead and there is no faith.

Chorus

I'm thinking in my own interest as much as yours, daughter.
If I am wrong, have it your own way.
We will never leave you.

Electra

Women, I am ashamed if I upset you with all this weeping.
Forgive me, I have to do it, I have to.
Could any woman with good blood in her veins do otherwise?
I see the suffering in my father's house.
I see that suffering day and night.

It gets worse, not better.
First, look at myself and the mother who bore me—
I hate her.
Then look at me living in my own home with my
father's killers.
They rule me.
They decide if I get or I go without.
How do you think I survive the days when I see him,
I see Aegisthus sitting on my father's throne?
He wears every stitch my father wore.
He pours wine on the same fire where he murdered.
And the worst—what is worse—
I see my father's bed, and his killer lies beside my
mother.
Mother—is that a fit name for such a woman?
She is so depraved she lives with that obscenity.
She fears no force of retribution.
It's as if she's gloating over what she's done.
She celebrates the date her treachery killed my
father.
Cattle are slaughtered, and they dance.
Every month she gives sacrifice to the gods that
protect her.
And I am the unfortunate woman, alone in the house,
Lamenting, wasting away, looking at this
abomination,
Weeping at the feast they call after my father.
And I am not allowed to cry my heart's content.
That gracious woman gives full vent to her insulting
tongue.
'You are full of hate, girl, you're accursed.
Have you and you alone lost a father?
Has no one else ever known grief?

May your death be sore and the gods damn you.'
That's how she insults me, and then she hears
Orestes will return.
She works herself into a thundering rage, she roars,
'You are the cause of this, aren't you?
You stole Orestes from my arms, you smuggled him
away,
You will pay the hard price you deserve.'
She's foaming these words like a mad dog,
And her noble husband stands urging her on,
That complete coward, that deadly scourge,
A man letting his woman fight his battles.
And I will turn to dust waiting for Orestes;
Come back, put an end to this, or I will die in
misery.
I hear he's coming, then he does not come,
And so he's destroyed whatever hope I dared
hope.
My friends, that is how I lead my life.
There's nothing holy anymore, nothing sane nor
sensible.
The world's turned bad, and so have I.

Chorus

Tell me, are you saying this when Aegisthus is in the
house?
Is he away from home?

Electra

Of course he's away.
I would not set foot outside the door if he were
inside.
He is in the country.

Chorus

If that's so, I'd press you further.

Electra

It's so. Ask what you want to ask.

Chorus

Your brother—will he come or not?
I want to know.

Electra

He says that he will come.
He does none of the things he says he will do.

Chorus

A man takes his time when he's to do a great deed.

Electra

I did not take my time when I saved him.

Chorus

You know his heart is good—he will help his friends.

Electra

I believe it, or else I could not stay alive.

Chorus

Say no more for I see your sister, Chrysothemis,
Your full sister from the same father and same mother.
She's carrying offerings from the house to give to the dead.

(*Chrysothemis enters*)

Chrysothemis

What are the things you are saying outside the house, sister?
After so long lamenting, will you not learn you are wasting your time?
Your anger's useless.
I know well enough, how bad our way of life is.
I also know what my feelings are.
If I'd power, I'd tell our masters.
But these are dangerous waters and we must move carefully.
Nothing I do must threaten them.
I want you to do the same.
I know you have justice on your side, and I do not.
But they have power.
I must obey them in everything if I'm to be a free woman.

Electra

You are your father's daughter, and you should be ashamed.
You forget him because you respect your mother.
You lecture me with what you learnt from her.
You do not have a word to say for yourself.
You make your choice.
You be foolish, like me, or you be wise and forget your own.
You said if you had power they would feel your hatred.
You then betray me when I do all I can to honour my father.
You try to stop me.
You'd be a coward as well as a victim, would you?

You teach me or you listen to me:
What would it profit me to stop mourning?
Do I not have a life?
A miserable life, but it is enough for me.
And if I harm them, then it is an honour,
A pleasure for the dead if the dead feel pleasure.
You say that you hate them, but it's only a word, your hatred.
You live among them, you live with your father's killers.
Well, the earth will cover me before I give in to them,
Not if they were to give me your pomp and your pleasures.
You eat yourself full and your life is a leisure.
What I eat does not sicken my stomach.
I have no desire to enjoy your privilege.
You would not either if you were thinking rightly.
You could be called the daughter of the greatest of men.
You choose, as things stand, to be your mother's child.
You are what you seem to be—a traitor.
You have betrayed your dead father.
You have betrayed your own.

Chorus

Please, say nothing in anger.
There's wisdom on both sides.
Learn from her, and she learns from you.

Chrysothemis

I've grown used to her way of talking.

I would not have broken breath but that I did learn something.
She is facing great danger.
That will put a stop to her lamenting.

Electra

Great danger—what is it? Come on, tell me.
If it's worse than what I now endure, I will not say another word.

Chrysothemis

Then I'll tell you all I know.
They will lock you away from the light of the sun if you don't stop lamenting.
You will be taken away from this country.
You will be buried alive in a dungeon and left to mourn there.
Take stock of that, and don't blame me afterwards.
You have the chance to show some sense.

Electra

They have decided to do that to me?

Chrysothemis

When Aegisthus comes home, yes.

Electra

Then let him come home soon.

Chrysothemis

You are crazed—what curse are you putting on yourself?

Electra
Let him come, if these things you say he has in mind—

Chrysothemis
May happen to you? What kind of madness makes
you want—

Electra
To get away as far as possible from you all.

Chrysothemis
You do not care to leave the life you lead now?

Electra
Yes, the life I lead now is wonderfully agreeable.

Chrysothemis
It would be, if you had some logic—

Electra
And is it your logic to be disloyal to my own?
Is that what you teach me?

Chrysothemis
I am not trying to teach you that, but to bow the knee
to those in power.

Electra
You can bow the knee, I will stand upright.

Chrysothemis
Honour demands you do not come to grief through
being stubborn and stupid.

Electra

My father's honour, I will defend, and if I must, I will come to grief.

Chrysothemis

But our father does not demand this. He will forgive us this—I know.

Electra

The words of a coward, and you said them.

Chrysothemis

Will you not stand with me and say them too?

Electra

No. I am not so stupid.

Chrysothemis

Then I will go about my own business.

Electra

Where are you going? Why are you carrying those offerings?

Chrysothemis

For my father's grave—my mother sent me with them.

Electra

What are you saying?
She's making offerings at the grave of her worst enemy?

Chrysothemis

To the man she murdered, is that what you mean?

Electra

Who persuaded her to do this? Who approved of this?

Chrysothemis

I believe she had a terrible dream.

Electra

My father and my father's father, may your gods help me at last.

Chrysothemis

Do you find some hope in terror?

Electra

I can tell you that if you can tell me about her dream.

Chrysothemis

I know very little.

Electra

Tell me.
Very little may be enough to swing fate in our favour.

Chrysothemis

They say our father came back to life.
He returned to the light of day.
The sceptre he used to carry, the one Aegisthus carries now,
My father took it and planted it beside the fire.
It grew into a bough thick with fruit.

It cast its shadow over all Mycenae.
She told her dream to the Sun.
Someone near her heard and told me this story.
It is her fear makes her send me to the grave.
I know no more.
I beg you, by all the gods we believe in, do as I say.
Stop this foolishness or you'll come to great harm.
If you cast me aside, you'll come to me regretting it.

Electra

My dear sister, leave nothing on the tomb.
That woman hated our father.
Neither God nor man would let her honour his grave.
Give them to the wind.
Hide them deep in the dust.
They won't disturb where my father lies dead.
Save them for herself when death takes her.
She is so without shame she dares to pray for the man she murdered.
Do you think the man dead in the earth will receive her offerings?
She dishonoured him in death.
She killed him like an enemy.
She cut his corpse to ribbons.
And she wiped the blood off her hands on his head.
Do you believe these offerings will clear her of the murder?
That cannot be.
Get rid of them.
Go to our father's grave and cut a lock from your hair.
Take this tangled one from my unhappy head.
It's very little, but it's all I have.

My belt too, it's a poor thing, but give them to him.
Kneel and pray that in his kindness,
He comes from beneath and helps us scatter our enemies.
Pray that he'll come and destroy all who stand against us.
Someday we may make him richer offerings than they do now.
I do believe—I truly believe this—
He sent these terrible dreams to her.
Sister, do this and you will help us both,
You will help the most loved of all men.
Our father, our dead father.

Chorus

Her words are holy.
Dear girl, if you're wise, do as she says.

Chrysothemis

It's my duty, I'll do it.
There will be no argument.
But if you care about me, good women,
Say nothing about what I'm doing.
If my mother hears of it, it will be on my head.

(*Chrysothemis exits*)

Chorus

May I not bear false witness,
But through the darkness,
I see the workings of Justice.
She knows what has to be.

She will plant her fatal kiss
On the lips of your enemies.
And soon she will be here.
My mind is dancing.
That dream's destroyed my fears.
I heard that and my heart took wing.
Your father, leader of the Greeks,
He will always remember,
And the axe that bloodied his brave cheek
Waits the call from its bronze lair.
Bronze too are the terrible claws
Of the god who devours the lawless.
She has seen the bed where adulterers sleep,
Seen the wedding clothes, the wedding feast,
And her gift will be a pit so deep
No cry of comfort from man nor beast
Shall reach their ears who did the deed
And sinned against the mighty gods.
It's clear as day for all to read
Revenge will never spare the rod.
If there's no truth in that woman's dream,
Our prayers are lost and dying screams.
The founder of this house,
Pelops, long ago,
You began this sorrow.
Thrown from his chariot,
Martilus died, brought
Down by your deceit,
And sorrows meet
With sorrow since in this unhappy house.

(*Clytemnestra enters*)

Clytemnestra

So you're prowling outside the house again,
It's easy seeing Aegisthus is not here.
At least he stops you shaming your family in the eye of the world.
Now he's away you show me no respect.
Your constant refrain is that I'm cruel,
That I do great harm to you and yours.
I am not a cruel woman.
But I do abuse you because you abuse me so often.
And your excuse is your father, nothing else.
I killed him.
I know it well.
I do not deny it.
But I did not act alone.
Justice killed him too.
If you'd come to your senses, you would be on her side.
Tell me, this father of yours that you're constantly lamenting,
Tell me why he and he alone among the Greeks,
Why did he sacrifice your sister to the gods?
His child that he had the pleasure to conceive—
I had the pain to give her birth.
Tell me why he did this, explain.
For whose sake did he sacrifice her?
For the Greeks, would you say?
But they have no right to kill her.
She was mine. My child.
And if it was for his brother, Menelaus, that he killed her,
Should he not have paid the penalty to me?
He cut her soft white throat, my Iphigenia. My child.

If I had touched Orestes, he would have killed me.
He killed my daughter—why should he not die?
Menelaus had two children.
They ought to have died, not mine.
Was it not for their father and mother that this war started?
Did death want to grow fat on my children, not hers?
Did your damned father feel pity for the children of Menelaus?
Had he no pity for mine?
I killed him—I made the only choice I could.
Your father was a fool, he was insane.
That's what she would say, if she could still speak,
My dead daughter.
And I do not regret what was done.
And were you dead, you would have demanded I did the deed.
Before you judge me, judge yourself.
Are you so sure of the ground you stand on?

Electra

This time, don't accuse me of starting the quarrel.
But if you deign to listen, I want to tell the truth,
The truth about my father and my sister.

Clytemnestra

I allow that.
If you had always spoken so civilly, I would have listened more to you.

Electra

Then listen now.
You say that you killed my father.

Whether you acted justly or not, what greater crime could you admit to?
And I tell you that you did not kill him in the name of Justice.
You acted under the influence of an evil man.
And you are now living with him.
Ask Artemis, the goddess of the hunt, why she stilled the winds in Aulis?
No, let me tell you, because we cannot question her. She is a goddess.
They say my father was hunting in a grove sacred to the divinity.
He startled a deer, a dappled, horned stag.
When he killed the animal, she heard him boasting,
And in her anger, Artemis detained our ships.
A sacrifice had to be made: his daughter for the beast.
That is how she went to her death.
There was no other way for the army to go home or get to Troy.
That is why he sacrificed her.
It was against his will, and with great suffering.
It was not done for the sake of Menelaus.
But say you're right, say he had done it to help him,
Was that a reason for him to die at your hands?
Whose law is that?
You watch when you lay down the law.
You may be laying down your own pain and punishment.
If you were to get what you deserve,
If we are to take a life for a life,
You should die first.

The excuse you make for yourself does not excuse
you.
Tell me this.
Why are you bedding the man who killed my father?
He is guilty.
You give him children.
You cast aside your older children—
We fear God because our father feared God,
So I do not excuse your adultery.
Or do you say that too is for your dead daughter?
If you do, then it is beyond shame.
You sleep with a dire enemy for your daughter's
sake.
I'm wasting my breath talking to you.
You say all I do is abuse my mother.
Mother.
No—you torture me.
You torture us all.
I lead an unhappy life.
I live with the constant cruelty you and your mate
pour on me.
And another child wears himself away in exile.
Orestes.
He barely escaped from your bloodstained hands.
You've often accused me that I saved him to make
you suffer.
Well, know this.
If I'd had the power, I would have done so.
Tell that to the world.
If you think me wicked, arrogant, shameless—
good.
That proves me worthy to be your breed.

Chorus

There's a fire in her head.
It's burning her up. She's not just.
She doesn't care what she's saying.

Clytemnestra

What should I care about her? She has so insulted her mother.
She's a grown woman.
Will she stop at nothing—has she no shame?

Electra

Yes, I do feel shame, even if you might not think so.
I know what I'm doing's wrong—
It goes against my nature.
But you are malign, you are cruel.
You force me to act against my will.
And if I shock you, you've taught me how to.

Clytemnestra

You are a disgrace.
All I say and do gives you more ammunition.

Electra

All you say, all you do is your doing and saying.
You find the words fit for what you do.

Clytemnestra

I swear by Artemis you will face Aegisthus when he's home.

Electra

Please, offer your sacrifice.

Don't let me stop you.
I will say no more.

Clytemnestra

Raise up my offerings of the fruits of the earth.
I pray to the Lord to lift my terrible fears.
Phoebus Apollo, my protector, listen to my heart's secret.
I am not among friends.
I cannot speak openly while she stands near me.
Her hatred and bitter words would spread lies through the city.
Listen to me, and hear my secret.
Great Apollo, two visions came in dreams last night.
If they bode well, fulfil them.
But if they are bad omens, turn them against my enemies.
If some plan to rob me of the wealth I possess, prevent them.
Let me live a life unharmed.
Let me rule the house of Atreus and this kingdom.
Let me live among friends.
Let my days be prosperous.
Let the children who wish me no pain prosper too.
God Apollo, hear me kindly.
Give to me and mine what we pray for.
There is more that I want, but cannot say.
You are a god, and you know well what it is.
The children of Zeus see everything.

(*An old Servant enters*)

Servant
Women of Mycenae, is this the house of Aegisthus?

Chorus
It is, stranger, you've guessed right.

Servant
Am I right to guess this lady is his wife?
She has the look of a queen.

Chorus
That is the very lady.

Servant
Great lady, I bring good news from a friend to you
and Aegisthus.

Clytemnestra
I welcome you, but want to know who sent you.

Servant
Phanoteus, and it concerns an important matter.

Clytemnestra
You come from a friend and your words will be
friendly.
What is this important matter?

Servant
Orestes is dead.

(*Electra howls*)

Clytemnestra

What are you saying?
Pay no heed to her.
What are you saying, stranger?

Servant

I said, Orestes is dead. I say—

Electra

Orestes is dead, and I am no more.

Clytemnestra

Be quiet.
Are you telling me the truth, stranger?
How did he die?

Servant

That is what I've come to tell you.
He came with the pride of Greece to the Delphic
    Games.
When the first race was proclaimed he entered—
A magnificent man, admired by all eyes.
He ran as well as he looked, he won the great prize.
No other man enjoyed such triumphs—
He won victory in each and every contest.
Great cheers went to heaven.
Orestes, the Greek, has won.
The son of Agamemnon, the leader against Troy.
That's how things went, but if the gods are up to
    badness,
Even the mightiest man will fall.
The next day, at sunrise, the chariots would race.

He entered the lists with many others.
The first was an Achaen, the second a Spartan,
Two came from Libya, skilled charioteers.
Orestes came next, his mares from Thessaly.
The sixth, with chestnut colts, hailed from Aetolia.
The seventh was Magnesian, and the eighth, an
Aenian, had white horses.
The ninth came from Athens, built by the gods,
And the last was Boeotian, filling the tenth chariot.
The umpires drew lots and signed each his place.
The brazen trumpets sound, and the chariots start.
The reins are tight, the steeds are ready, they shout,
And the whole course is the clash of rattling chariots.
The dust is rising, and they nearly collide.
For each man goaded on the creatures before him;
Each wished to pass the wheels and the others'
panting steeds.
The horses' breath has turned to foam,
They drenched the drivers' backs and wheels.
Orestes kept his horses near the pillar,
He grazed the post, he checked his pursuer.
And so it continues, they are all unscathed,
But beware the milk-white hard-mouthed Aenian
steeds,
They bolt between the sixth and seventh round,
They dash their brains against the Barcaean chariot.
One driver crashes into another's path,
And the wreckage covers the whole plain of Crisa.
The driver from Athens, he knows his stuff,
He slackens, stops, he draws aside,
The surge of chariots in complete confusion.
Orestes stays in the rear, he's trusting in the finish,
He sees the Athenian alone is left,

He gives a roar to the racing horses, they rush on,
They bring their chariots together, they're level,
First one, then the other is in front.
Orestes kept his nerve, the horses kept on course,
Then, as the horses turned, his left hand relaxed,
Before he knew it he struck the pillar's edge.
The axle box breaks, he slides over the rail,
He falls to the ground, the horses mad in the middle
of the course.
And a cry of pity rises for the young man,
So brave and so bloody his end,
Flung to the earth, his feet soaring to the sky.
The drivers with great difficulty stopped their
horses.
They free his corpse—no friend would know him,
Disfigured, dirty with blood.
They buried him on a funeral pyre, the Phoceans.
This magnificent man, now miserable dust,
They poured into an urn to carry to his home.
That is the terrible story I have to tell you.
For those who saw it with their own eyes,
There was never a sadder sight.

Chorus

Our ancient house is over, destroyed root and
branch.

Clytemnestra

Oh God, what is this?
Is it fortunate or terrible?
Do I gain from it?
It troubles me that I keep my life through my great
loss.

Servant

Lady, why are you downhearted at my news?

Clytemnestra

Giving birth is strange.
You do not hate your children, no matter how they treat you.

Servant

Then my coming here was in vain.

Clytemnestra

No, not in vain—do not say in vain.
Do you have proof that he is dead,
The son I gave birth to?
I nurtured him at my breast, but in exile he turned from me.
He left this land and never saw me,
He blamed me for his father's murder,
He swore revenge against me.
Sweet sleep never closed my eyes day nor night since,
I live like a woman condemned to die.
This day I have been freed from fear,
The fear of him and that woman there.
She was a worse torture.
She lived in my house, draining my life blood,
But now I'll pass my days in peace for all her threats.

Electra

Orestes!
I can lament your fate.
Your mother mocks it.
Am I not well off?

Clytemnestra

No, but he is, where he is.

Electra

Nemesis, Goddess of Revenge, hear what she's said of her son.

Clytemnestra

Nemesis has heard what she needed to hear.
She's made up her own mind.

Electra

Mock me—you are the winner in this.

Clytemnestra

Then will you and Orestes put a stop to this?

Electra

It's we who have been stopped, not us stopping you.

Clytemnestra

Stranger, if you had silenced that roaring mouth,
You would have been well rewarded.

Servant

If all is well, then may I leave?

Clytemnestra

No, you deserve a better welcome.
Come in, leave her to lament.
She and her friends have plenty to cry over.

(*Clytemnestra and the Servant enter the palace*)

Electra

Do you think that creature weeps for her son in pain and grief?
No, she is gloating.
Orestes!
Orestes, by your death I die as well.
I have lost my last hope.
You would come and revenge my father and myself.
Now where can I go?
I have lost you and my father.
Now I must serve those I hate most,
The murderers of my father.
Do you call that justice?
No, I'll never darken their door again.
I'll walk out that gate and die alone.
If they loathe me, let them kill me.
To die would be a pleasure, to survive would be pain—
I have no wish to live.

Chorus

Zeus, where are your bolts of thunder?
Where is the fire of the sun?
Can they look now and not see this?

(*Electra howls in pain*)

Daughter, do not cry.

(*Electra howls again*)

Do not weep so loudly.

Electra

You are tearing my heart in two.

Chorus

How do we do that?

Electra

Don't breathe a word of hope that he who's dead is still alive.
Do that and you dance on my breaking heart.

Chorus

A woman's golden necklace brought down King Amphiaraus,
And now beneath the earth—

Electra

This pain—

Chorus

He lives, warm and well—

Electra

Great pain—

Chorus

Great pain came to her—her—

Electra

His killer!

Chorus

Yes.

Electra

I know, I know.
But Amphiaraus had his champion.

I too had one, now snatched from me.

Chorus

Your heart is sore, so is your fate.

Electra

I know that too well.
My life is a river.
It floods with grief.
And it never stops, this flood.

Chorus

We have watched your tears fall.

Electra

Then let them still fall.
Give me no hope nor comfort.
My brother is dead.

Chorus

All men die.

Electra

To die as he did, a poor young man?
Tangled in the reins, beneath the horse's brutal
hooves?

Chorus

Do not think of the horror.

Electra

To die among strangers—I could not touch him—

(*The Chorus howls with pain*)

He was put in the earth.
We gave him no funeral.
We shed no tears over him.

(*Chrysothemis enters*)

Chrysothemis
Dear sister, I raced here to give you great news.
It will bring an end to all your suffering.

Electra
An end to all my suffering?
There is neither relief nor remedy.

Chrysothemis
Orestes is here—
Do you know what I'm saying?
Orestes is here, just as I am here.

Electra
Sister, are you mad?
Are you mocking me and yourself?

Chrysothemis
I swear by my father I'm not mocking.
I'm telling you we have him here.

Electra
No, it's not so.
Who has told this story that you believe so easily?

Chrysothemis
I believe it because I saw the signs with my own eyes.
I didn't hear it from another soul.

Electra

What have you seen that proves it?
What evidence have you?
What madness is in your mind?

Chrysothemis

Listen and learn from me, then say if I'm mad.

Electra

Speak on, if that will please you.

Chrysothemis

Then I'll tell you all I saw.
I approached my father's grave, there were streams of milk flowing,
And round the urn a garland of every kind of flower.
I was astounded, and looked about me.
Was someone watching?
Nothing stirred, no one, so I crept nearer the tomb,
And there at the grave's edge—a fresh-cut lock of hair.
And my soul knew—it saw Orestes.
Orestes!
An omen, a sign from the one I love most in this world.
I took it in my hands, I couldn't speak,
My eyes were crying tears of joy.
I knew it then, I knew for certain.
This precious offering was his.
Who else but you or me could put it there?
I swear to you, it was not my doing, nor yours.
How could it be you?
You cannot leave the house even to worship.
Was it our mother then?

That is not her way.
And she could not have done it without us noticing.
It is Orestes.
These offerings at the tomb came from him.
Dear sister, have courage.
We are not always victims of the same fate.
We've had our share of bad fortune.
Maybe today it's turning to good.

Electra

Good girl, I pity your innocent wit.

Chrysothemis

Is my news not good news?

Electra

You're living in the land of dreams, and you don't
know it.

Chrysothemis

How can I not know what I saw with my two eyes?

Electra

He is dead, my poor girl.
Don't look to a dead man for salvation.
That chance is gone.

Chrysothemis

No.
Who told you this?

Electra

From a man who saw him meet his fate.

Chrysothemis

What man—where?
I cannot fathom this.

Electra

He is inside with our mother.
Her welcome was not cold.

Chrysothemis

No—no.
Who left the wreathes—who poured the milk onto the grave?

Electra

Someone kind has left offerings to our dead Orestes.

Chrysothemis

And I was the poor fool rushing here with good news.
I did not know our pitiful plight.
Now I find new sorrows added to our old.

Electra

That is how things stand.
Listen to me now.
You will lighten the load of the burden we carry.

Chrysothemis

How can I make the dead rise?

Electra

That is not what I said—I am not insane.

Chrysothemis

Then what can I do—what are you asking?

Electra

You must bring yourself to do what I advise.

Chrysothemis

If I can do it, I will.

Electra

Remember—to succeed you must put your shoulder to the work.

Chrysothemis

I know that, and I'll use all my strength.

Electra

Then listen to what I am determined to do.
You know as well as I do we've no friends here.
Death has robbed us blind, we two are alone.
While my brother lived and prospered, I had hopes
He would appear and avenge his father.
Now that he's dead, I'm turning to you.
You are my sister, I need a sister's help.
We must murder—don't back away—
We must murder our father's murderer.
Kill Aegisthus.
Now I've spelt it out for you.
Why hesitate?
What hope have you to look forward to?
You have been cheated of your inheritance.
Will you watch your life withering away?
Will you live unloved, with no wedding bed?
Don't dream married bliss is in store for you.
Aegisthus is not that stupid a man.

He won't risk his destruction from your child or
mine.
Take my advice and you will profit handsomely.
Your name, to our dead father, our brother too,
Your name will be holy to them.
You will show yourself to be a free-born woman.
You will marry well—
A worthy woman delights all men.
Consent—
Do you see the honour together we will win?
What friend or stranger will not greet us with praise?
They'll cry, 'Look at the two sisters!
They saved their father's house.
They looked their enemy in the eye,
They avenged murder.
Love them, revere them,
At every feast honour their bravery.'
Our name will be celebrated far and wide,
Our glory will live after death.
Sweet sister, work with your father,
Side with your brother,
Save me from my sorrows and save yourself.
Remember this.
Shame is truly shame to a noble soul.

Chorus

In matters like these it's wise to be cautious—
Both of you, be cautious.

Chrysothemis

If she had an ounce of sense in her, before she
opened her mouth,

She would have exercised caution but, good women,
she doesn't.
Just who do you imagine that you are—
Full of fighting talk and I'm to follow you?
You are a woman, not a man—do you know that?
You are no match against those against you.
They have the good fortune, we the bad.
They're on the rise and we are sinking.
Who would battle with such a mighty man?
If you do, you will be eaten without salt.
If anyone's heard your words, we're in deeper
trouble.
What good is glory? If we die in disgrace?
Dying is easy—
But locked up longing for death, and being denied it,
That is beyond shame.
I beg you, before we wreck ourselves entirely,
Restrain your anger.
All you've said to me will be breath wasted.
You are powerless, they have power, learn to give in.

Chorus

Listen to her, Electra.
Think of the future, go easy, you must.

Electra

Just as I imagined.
Before you opened your mouth I knew you'd turn
your back.
I'll stand alone and I myself will do it.
Though I'm on my own, it will be done, because it
must be.

Chrysothemis

Good for you.
It's a pity you weren't so determined when father
died.
What would you have done then?

Electra

My spirit was the same, but my head was not ready.

Chrysothemis

Try to keep that head on your shoulders still.

Electra

I take it you refuse to help me?

Chrysothemis

I do, because you will fail.

Electra

You're wise, well done—you're a coward, damn you.

Chrysothemis

You condemn me now, you'll praise me later,
I'll listen to them one and the same.

Electra

You'll never listen to praise from me.

Chrysothemis

Time will tell—we'll see.

Electra

Get from my sight—you're useless to me.

Chrysothemis
Unless I'm not—but you won't listen or learn.

Electra
Run to your mother—tell her all about it.

Chrysothemis
I do not hate you that much.

Electra
But you do not respect me, I know.

Chrysothemis
Not respect you? I want to help you.

Electra
So you decide what is right and wrong?

Chrysothemis
When you return to reason, I'll follow you.

Electra
Very wise you are, and very wrong.

Chrysothemis
My words to you exactly.

Electra
Do you not think what I say is right?

Chrysothemis
Sometimes being right is wrong.

Electra

I will not live with such a lie.

Chrysothemis

If you do this, you'll see that I was right.

Electra

I will do it, and I won't be swayed by you.

Chrysothemis

Is that really so—will you not think again?

Electra

No—nothing is worse than wrong advice.

Chrysothemis

You're deaf to every word I argue.

Electra

I decided this long ago.

Chrysothemis

I'll leave you to it.
My words won't turn you from your ways.

Electra

Run along inside.
Even if you begged me, I'd not listen to you.
It's insane to ask for what's impossible to get.

Chrysothemis

If you think you're wise, then so be it.
Your heart will soon be sore that you did not hear my
words.

(*Chrysothemis exits*)

Chorus

Consider the birds of the air.
In their fragile nest they sustain
Those who gave them life and pleasure.
So should we pay to those of our name
That debt, that bond of nature.
As God is just, guardian of all laws,
No mortal escapes punishment.
The day of judgement dawns.
O voice that's truly heaven sent,
Tell this to the dead below,
Tell Agamemnon this great sorrow,
His house is standing desolate.
The ties of blood are torn.
Where once was love there now is hatred.
Alone, Electra mourns.
She weeps for her poor father
Like a bird who's lost its child.
She looks upon his killers,
And her heart is driven wild.
Where shall you find on this earth
A woman to match her worth?
The wisest, best of daughters,
Electra mourns alone.
She waits for her glory till stone
Turns to water.
May I see you in that glory,
May I see your blood restored.
Your fate will change, it will come good,
You feared God's law, and you feared God.

(*Orestes and Pylades enter*)

Orestes

Tell me, women, are we on the right road to our destination?

Chorus

What are you looking for—why are you here?

Orestes

I've been looking a long time for the home of Aegisthus.

Chorus

You've come the right way—it's here.

Orestes

Could you tell them we have arrived?
They have long been waiting for us.

Chorus

This young woman should do that—she's related to them.

Orestes

Lady, tell them some Phocians are looking for Aegisthus.

Electra

Don't tell me you've come with proof positive of the story we've heard.

Orestes

What story?
I was told to bring news about Orestes.

Electra

What news?
I'm shaking with fear.

Orestes

He's dead.
This small urn—it contains all that's left of him.

Electra

I see it with my own unhappy eyes.
I see the burden you carry, my burden.

Orestes

Are you weeping for Orestes?
This is his dust.

Electra

If those are his ashes, give me that to hold.
I'll weep for that dust, and for myself.
I'll weep for my whole family.

Orestes

Give this to her.
She means no harm to it.
She's a friend to him, or one of his family.

Electra

Orestes, the man I loved most,
This is all that is left of you.
I sent you away from here, full of hope,
But your return has emptied all hope from me.
Now you are nothing,
And I hold you in my hands,
But the day you left, you were the light of day.

I wish I had died before I saved you from death.
I sent you into a foreign land.
You could have fallen here beside your father,
You could have lain with him in his grave.
But you died in exile, far from home, from your
sister.
It was a sad death.
I was not there.
I could not wash your lovely corpse with my hands.
I could not snatch your lovely bones from the pyre.
Strangers' hands buried you.
You come back to me as dust, a handful of dust.
I nursed you as a baby, I didn't mind the bother,
You were never your mother's child, you were mine.
No one else in that house cared for you but me.
You called me sister—sister you called me.
All vanished in a day, dead with your death.
The wind's come and blown everything away.
Your father's dead, and I'm dead, and you're lost.
Those who stand against us laugh.
Your mother, who is no mother, is mad with joy.
Her crimes, I know, you would have put a stop to
them.
But fate is cruel, your fate and mine.
It does not bring me your beautiful face.
No, it delivers cold ash and useless shadow.
Pain—
Pain—
Pain—
Pain—
Pain—
You have destroyed me, my loved, loved brother,
Yes, you have destroyed me.

Zoë Wanamaker as Electra and Myra Lucretia Taylor as Chorus.

Take me with you.
I am nothing, let me turn into nothing with you.
We live as one together on this earth.
Now I want to die with you in the grave.
For the dead do not mourn, they do not mourn.

Chorus

Electra, child, you are mortal,
Your father and Orestes too—mortal.
Death comes to us all.
We have to face it.

Orestes

What can I say?
I cannot speak, but I can no longer hold my tongue.

Electra

Why do you say that—what's wrong with you?

Orestes

Am I looking at the great woman, Electra?

Electra

That is me, and I'm a sorry sight.

Orestes

Yours is a pitiful story. So pitiful.

Electra

Sir, your pity is not for me, surely.

Orestes

Your beauty has been broken and wickedly
disfigured.

Electra

Yes, sir, I am the woman your words describe.

Orestes

They stopped you from marrying—they've
sentenced you to misery.

Electra

Stranger, why do you look at me and lament?

Orestes

I've known so little of my own sorrow.

Electra

What have I said to tell you that?

Orestes

Because you are marked by many sorrows.

Electra

You see only half of them.

Orestes

What worse pain could there be than this?

Electra

To live with murderers.

Orestes

Whose murderers?
What evil are you whispering about?

Electra

My father's, and I am their slave.

Orestes
Who demands this?

Electra
My mother, who is mother only in name.

Orestes
What does she do?
Is she violent, does she deprive you—

Electra
She is violent—she deprives me—

Orestes
Is there no one to help you prevent it?

Electra
There was one—you've shown me his ashes.

Orestes
Poor girl, for a long time I've looked at you with pity.

Electra
You are the first who has ever pitied me.

Orestes
I am the first to know your pain is my pain.

Electra
Who are you—some relative from far away?

Orestes
If these women are on our side, I can tell you.

Electra

They're with us, you can trust them.

Orestes

Give me back that urn, and I'll tell you everything.

Electra

Please, stranger, don't ask me to do that.

Orestes

Do as I say, you won't regret it.

Electra

Don't take what I love most in this life.

Orestes

I won't let you keep it.

Electra

My loved Orestes, I cannot even bury you.

Orestes

Be quiet—you have no reason to weep.

Electra

No reason to weep—my brother's dead!

Orestes

You have no right to call him that.

Electra

Do you refuse to let me respect the dead?

Orestes

You are refused nothing, but this doesn't belong to you.

Electra

It does, if this is my brother's body.

Orestes

It is not him. It is not Orestes.

Electra

Then where is his grave?

Orestes

There is none—we don't bury the living.

Electra

Son, what are you saying?

Orestes

All I say is true.

Electra

Is the man alive?

Orestes

Alive as I am.

Electra

Orestes—is it you?

Orestes

My father's signet ring—am I telling the truth?

(*Electra gives a cry of joy, matched by Orestes*)

Electra

Do I hear your voice again?

Orestes

My voice—none other.

Electra

Do I hold you in my arms?

Orestes

Hold me there for ever.

Electra

Dear woman, dear friend, look—it's Orestes.
We thought him dead—know now he's alive.

Chorus

Daughter, we see him and we're crying for your good fortune.

Electra

My darling, darling son, you've come home.
You're here, you've arrived, you've seen those you love.

Orestes

I'm here but sssh—wait.

Electra

What's wrong?

Orestes

It's best to keep quiet in case anyone in there should hear.

Electra

I swear by the Virgin I fear no one in that house.
Those women are good for nothing.
They're a waste of space on this earth.

Orestes

Women can fight as well.
You know that from experience.

Electra

Oh, you've brought back the old sorrow,
Never hide it—nothing can heal it—never forget it.

Orestes

I know that as well.
But the hour is coming.
We'll remember what they did.

Electra

I could tell what they did till the end of time.
My lips have been long sealed, now they're free.

Orestes

True, but mind how freely you speak.

Electra

Why?

Orestes
Don't say too much until the time is right.

Electra
Who could be silent? Who could say nothing?
I've seen you.
I never thought—I gave up hope.

Orestes
You see me here because the gods told me to come now.

Electra
If the gods brought you here, this is their greatest gift.
And in your being here, I see the hand of heaven.

Orestes
I don't want to limit your happiness, but it's too great—
You're frightening me.

Electra
I welcome you back with open arms, you're here,
You've seen how I was suffering, do not—

Orestes
Do not do what?

Electra
Take the light of day from me.
I find it in your face.

Orestes

Then find it there and in no other.

Electra

Do you allow me?

Orestes

I do.

Electra

Dear women, I've heard a voice I'd lost all hope of
hearing.
How could I be silent and not give one cry of joy?
I have you now.
I see your face, I'll see it for ever.
I'll never forget it.

Orestes

Say no more now.
I know how vile our mother is.
I know Aegisthus wastes our father's wealth.
This is not the time for these stories.
Tell me instead what we need to do.
Do we reveal ourselves, or do we lie in wait?
How do we wipe the smiles off our enemies' faces?
When we go inside,
Wipe the smile off your face.
Weep as if the tragic story were true.
When the battle's won, we'll have time to laugh.

Electra

Brother, I'll do everything to please you.
I would not harm you, even if it were to help myself.

The gods are on our side, I'll serve them.
You know how things stand here.
Aegisthus is not at home, our mother is in the house.
Don't worry, she won't see a smile on my face.
My hatred of her is too deep.
Since you've come back I've been weeping, weeping for joy.
On the one day I've seen you dead and alive.
How could I not weep?
It is a miracle.
If my father came back from the dead, I'd believe it.
Fate has guided you, so I'll do as you bid.
If I'd been left alone, I'd have done one of two things—
Live or die like a brave woman.

Orestes

Be quiet—I hear someone coming from the house.

(*The old Servant enters*)

Servant

Are you two complete fools?
Are you tired of living?
Have you not enough sense to see the danger you're steeped in?
I have been watching you, and it's just as well.
Those inside would have guessed what plot you're hatching.
As it is, I've taken care to prevent them doing so.
You've had your fill of welcomes and words of joy.
Get inside now.
Any more delay does us no good—make an end to this.

Orestes

When I go in, how shall I find things?

Servant

Everything's well—there's no chance they'll know you.

Orestes

You've told them I'm dead?

Servant

Here you're dead and in the grave.

Orestes

Are they pleased at that—what do they say?

Servant

I'll tell you all when you've settled this business.
Inside all is as well, or as wicked, as you'd expect.

Electra

Tell me, who is this, brother?

Orestes

Do you not see?

Electra

I have never set eyes on him.

Orestes

Do you not know the man into whose hands you
once put me?

Electra

What are you saying—what man?

Orestes

The man you trusted to carry me to Phocis.

Electra

This is the only one who stayed loyal to my murdered father?

Orestes

That's the man—let that be enough, ask no more questions.

Electra

This is a great day.
The one good man in Agamemnon's house—how have you come here?
Are you the man who saved us both from so many troubles?
I bless your hands, I bless your feet.
How could you be here so long without my knowing you?
Your news killed me, but the truth's brought me back to life.
I greet you as a father, for I think you are a father.
In one day I have hated and loved you like no other man.

Servant

That's enough for now.
There will be plenty of time to tell all, Electra.
But don't stand here—it's time to act, you two men.
Clytemnestra is alone,
There is no man inside.
If you hold back now, you'll face an army soon.

Orestes

No more time for words, Pylades,
Time to get inside.
First we'll pray to the gods that guard my father's
house.

(*Orestes, Pylades and the Servant enter the palace. Electra prays to the statue of Apollo*)

Electra

Lord Apollo, hear their prayer—hear mine also.
I've stood before you often.
I made you offerings from what little I possessed.
Now I ask, Lord Apollo, with all I have,
I fall before you, I implore you,
Let our work prosper,
Show to the godless how the gods reward evil.

Chorus

The God of War advances,
Breathing blood and vengeance.
The hounds are on the trail,
The sinners wait within.
My mind can see it all,
There's no escaping death.
The champion of the dead,
He's entered the house,
Ancestral hall of kings.
His sword is smelling blood.

Electra

Good women, say nothing, but the men will soon
finish the work.

Chorus

What are they doing?

Electra

They stand by her as she prepares the urn for burial.

Chorus

Why have you rushed out?

Electra

To watch in case Aegisthus surprises us.

(*Clytemnestra cries from within the palace*)

Clytemnestra

Is there none to help me?
Are you all killers?

Electra

Do you hear, friends—someone inside is crying out.

Chorus

I've heard that dreadful cry—it frightens me.

Clytemnestra

Aegisthus, where are you?

Electra

Listen—another cry.

Clytemnestra

Son—son—have mercy on your mother.

Electra

You had none for him nor the man who fathered him.

Chorus

My unhappy city, this unhappy house,
A curse was placed upon you.
Now it's being lifted.

Clytemnestra

You have struck me.

Electra

If you can, strike her again.

Clytemnestra

God help me—God help me.

Electra

I wish Aegisthus were with you.

Chorus

The curse has worked.
The dead live again,
Draining the blood of the living.

(*Orestes and Pylades enter from the palace*)

Chorus

Look—their hands are stained,
And I do not condemn them.

Electra

How have you fared, Orestes?

Orestes
I have done well, if Apollo spoke the truth.

Electra
Is that foul woman dead?

Orestes
Your mother will no longer displease you.

Chorus
Stop—I see Aegisthus coming.

Electra
Back into the house.

Orestes
Where do you see him?

Electra
Coming down the street.
He's smiling.
He is ours.

Chorus
Hurry into the palace.
You've done half your work well.
Now, finish it perfectly.

Orestes
We will—don't worry.

Electra
Get to where you're going.

Orestes

I'm on my way.

Electra

Leave matters here to me.

(*Orestes and Pylades exit*)

Chorus

Speak gently to him.
Let him walk blindly into the trap of Justice.

(*Aegisthus enters*)

Aegisthus

Can any tell me where the Phocian strangers are?
I've heard they say Orestes died falling from a chariot.
You—I'm asking you—you had enough to say before.
You have most to lose by this, so you should know.

Electra

Of course I know.
I should know what's happened to those I love most.

Aegisthus

Where are they—tell me immediately.

Electra

Inside—they've warmed the heart of their hostess.

Aegisthus

Do they truly say he was dead?

Electra

They did—they even showed us the dead man.

Aegisthus

May I see the body too—to make sure?

Electra

You may, but it's an ugly sight.

Aegisthus

For once, your words please me.

Electra

Stay pleased, if you've reason to be.

Aegisthus

Throw open the door.
Let all Mycenae and Argos see.
If you had hopes in this man, he is dead.
Now accept my rule—or face the dire consequences.

Electra

I've learnt my lesson.
Time's taught me to side with the strong.

(The doors open. There is a shrouded corpse with Orestes and Pylades beside it)

Aegisthus

Zeus, this man was laid low by the angry gods.
If that anger was justified, let me not say so.
Remove the covering from that face.
I must mourn for my relation.

Orestes

Remove it yourself.
You must look at this and speak kind words.

Aegisthus

Well said, I will.
Call Clytemnestra, if she is in the house.

Orestes

She is beside you—look.

(*Aegisthus lifts the covering. He starts in horror*)

Why are you frightened?
Don't you recognize the face?

Aegisthus

Who has set the trap that I've fallen into?

Orestes

Do you know you have been talking to the dead?

Aegisthus

Orestes—I understand—it's you.

Orestes

You are so deep, and yet so long deceived.

Aegisthus

You will kill me.
Let me say one thing—

Electra

Let him say nothing, brother, not one word.

He is doomed and let him die now.
Kill him, give his corpse to whoever will bury him.
Get him out of our sight.
Then and only then will I be rid of the wrongs he has done.

Orestes

Get inside.
Words won't save you—I want your life.

Aegisthus

Why do you force me into the house?
If what you're doing is right, why do it in darkness?
Why not kill me here?

Orestes

Give me no orders—get inside.

Aegisthus

Is this house forever cursed?
Shall there be killing after killing for ever?

Orestes

There shall be yours—that much I can see clearly.

Aegisthus

Then you see more than your father ever did.

Orestes

Your words are wasting my time.
Get inside.

Aegisthus

You lead the way.

Orestes

You go first.

Aegisthus

In case I run away?

Orestes

No—in case you choose where to die.
I want you to taste the bitterness of death.
Your sentence is swift and severe.

(*Aegisthus exits, followed by Orestes and Pylades*)

Chorus

Children of Atreus,
Your suffering has ended.
You have won freedom.
The deed is done.

COMMENTARY

Zoë Wanamaker was born in New York and raised and trained in London. Her career has spanned theatre, film, television and radio. She won her second "Best Actress" Olivier Award for this performance in 1997. Her first was for "May Daniels" in Trevor Nunn's production of *Once in a Lifetime,* for the Royal Shakespeare Company in 1979. Her other nominations are for *The Glass Menagerie* directed by Sam Mendes, which originated at the Donmar Warehouse; *The Importance of Being Earnest* directed by Sir Peter Hall; *The Day at Nice* and *Wrecked Eggs,* written and directed by Sir David Hare; *Mrs. Klein* directed by Peter Gill; *The Crucible* directed by Howard Davies (all for the National Theatre); *Twelfth Night, The Comedy of Errors, The Time of Your Life, Mother Courage,* and *Othello* (all for the Royal Shakespeare Company). She was also nominated for the premiere production of Arthur Miller's *The Last Yankee* (Young Vic). She has been nominated for two Tony Awards for her performances in *Piaf* (Plymouth), directed by Howard Davies, and *Loot* (Music Box), directed by John Tillinger. She starred in Anthony Minghella's *Made in Bangkok* (Mark Taper Forum) and has just completed a West End run of David Mamet's *The Old Neighborhood* (Royal Court), directed by Patrick Marber. Her starring roles on television include "Prime Suspect," "Love Hurts" (both BAFTA nominations), "Poor Little Rich Girl" (Golden Globe nomination), "Paradise Postponed," "Momento Mori," "The Countess Alice," "The Widowing of Mrs. Holroyd," "The Blackheath Poisonings," "The Edge of Darkness." Film credits include *The Hunger, Swept From the Sea,* and *Wilde* (BAFTA nomination). Ms. Wanamaker is an Honorary "Doctor of Letters" at the South Bank University and a trustee of Shakespeare's Old Globe Theatre in London.

Mark Glubke: I read an interview in which you said "Greek plays scare me . . . they make me feel stupid and unintelligent." That being the case, how did you come to play *Electra*?

Zoë Wanamaker: Actually (director) David (Leveaux) and I were working on *Suddenly Last Summer* and we were having lunch with Duncan Weldon, who was then director of the Chichester Festival Theater. Half way through lunch, David said, "Have you ever thought of doing *Electra*?" I said no and for that reason: because Greek drama made me feel unintelligent. I never understood them. To me, it was a bunch of people running around with masks and togas and a lot of moaning. I had also been asked to play Medea about four years previously. The first line in the play, Medea's entrance line, was "aye, aye, aye, aye, aye." And I thought "I couldn't do that . . . that would just make me laugh. I couldn't take that seriously. I didn't know where to even begin to experiment with making that sound." So, I rejected it. Then David said to me "I think it's about time you had a good scream" which was a very daunting thing for him to say. So, we went to a bookshop and we bought a translation of *Electra* and I looked at it. My first concern was that it had just been done about six years previously and I was frightened of being compared to that production. And then I thought to myself "there are a lot of people playing Hamlet, there are a lot of people playing Juliet, there are a lot of people performing all sorts of classic plays." Yet I quickly realized that if I did decide to do it, it would have to be adapted. And David said "I know just the person" and he asked Frank McGuinness. From what I am told, Frank went to the meeting with David prepared *not* to do it and then halfway through the meeting got very excited about the whole thing. And he finished the adaptation in six weeks. He works very fast. Of course, when I saw Frank's adaptation, I was convinced. What he had done is make *Electra* very colloquial. What I love about Frank's adaptation is he's pared Sophocles down to the fishbone. He's taken out the extraneous gods and goddesses. He's taken a lot of the words and adjectives that don't particularly matter and crystallized them down to the essential. That is the power of this adaptation: the nakedness of the language while at the same time retaining a wonderful sense of poetry. It's very bold, very powerful and, because of that, for me, it became a new play. There are a lot of "Frankisms" in it; there is one line that I know was his mother's. But he's made it accessible and direct and honest and clear. For an audience who doesn't know very much about Greek drama, it is startlingly modern. That's why I think it's brilliant.

MG: He's managed to pare down the language, yet push up the emotional quotient.

ZW: That's right.

MG: I think the audience feels this production more deeply than they have felt previous productions.

ZW: That's right. It's the simplicity of it. The simpler the better, I think. Simplicity is more powerful. You see that in painting, you see that in wonderful poetry, you see that in great writing. The sparity is much more powerful than all that other mess.

MG: Did you happen to see *A Doll's House*?

ZW: Yes, and I thought it also was very well done. What he did with *A Doll's House* was exactly the same thing: he made that much more modern, it went into the ear more easily, and the audience understood it more innately. I think that final scene particularly rang bells with the audience and I don't think that happens so strongly in other productions.

MG: Again, people felt something deeper than they usually feel.

ZW: And the same thing happens in *Electra*: the language that he's used has that direct simplicity and power. Having said that, I must tell you there are some classics scholars who fault the adaptation for not being literal enough. I've received a few letters from people who don't like it. One person took exception to the line "don't worry, you won't see a smile on my face." They then wrote out the actual translation into English and said they thought it was better. It was not better. It was crap to be perfectly honest. It was long and had no urgency, no reality at all compared to what Frank had done.

MG: Have you worked with Frank before?

ZW: Never. But we want to work together again.

MG: As you know, the reviews have been stunning. Many are calling this the performance of a lifetime. I am curious to know how you created this *Electra*.

ZW: I went to see a German production of *Electra*, the opera, and it was wild. The soprano was just sensational. I was impressed by the sheer physicality of the role . . . especially as played against that many violins in the orchestra. The moment when Clytemnestra is being killed, the violins are all screeching on a sustained note for a very long time. As a member of the audience, just to watch that is a theatrical, almost visceral experience. At the end of the production, when Clytemnestra is killed, blood started spurting from the set, pouring down this steel wall. Then, Electra danced in it and rolled in it! Now, *that* was just brilliant! For me, that was terribly exciting. Just the nakedness of that image and the horror of it. The dramatic power was just incredible. Then, I went to see De La Guarda, a group of aerialists from Argentina, who are just extraordinary. When they came to London, it was a real event. Their performance was sexy, powerful, political and remarkably energetic. So, those two productions greatly influenced me when I started working on *Electra*. I had those two images in my head. There was a physicality about this production that came to me. When I create a role, I usually do quite a bit of research. For this play, I did a little bit but I didn't go any further than I thought would be necessary for the bare essentials of this play. I wanted it to be completely new and fresh. To me, it's about a soul who is troubled, an avenging angel, a terrorist and yet a heroine of huge proportions. David's vision of it is that the play is about love, families, and the destruction of families. For me, it raises the question of what becomes of the children of war. What will become of those kids when they become twenty? What have we created?

MG: The piece David wrote for the *Playbill* was very well done. In it, he says a great play doesn't only capture its own era, but it serves as a prophecy for future generations. What do you think *Electra* has to say to our time?

ZW: I will say this: we are constantly confronted by the story of *Electra*. One example: in a few weeks time, the motion picture academy is going to give a lifetime achievement award to Elia Kazan. Now, for a lot of people, this is betrayal. He named names. He was the cause of many peoples' misery, the cause of their careers being taken away, the reason they were put in prison. Some people even committed suicide. Stories like this force us to confront what we would have done in the same situation. If we were German in the 1930s would we have become Nazis out of fear? If we were Jews, would we have escaped? Who knows. It is difficult to say unless you are in that situation. So, I really don't know what this play has to say to our time. What Sophocles offers us in *Electra* is a beautifully crafted piece of work. First, you meet Orestes and the tutor who tell you the story of what they plan to do. Then you meet Electra who is near death with grief. It's hatred that keeps her alive, if only just, and the hope that her brother will return. And then you meet her sister who has learned to compromise and who is the peacemaker. And then you meet the mother, whose child was murdered by Electra's father and, therefore, has another story. So, the audience then is confused. And that is where we are in society: constantly confused. Electra, however, is never confused about what she wants. But do we take that path of vengeance? If so, what does it do for us in the end? What does it do for Electra? What happens when vengeance has been wrought? Does it make her happy? Can she go on with her life? What does she become after that? So, it's difficult to say what *Electra* has to say to our time other than it raises all sorts of wonderful questions about ourselves. In this century, we have seen ourselves more nakedly than we have the courage to admit and we have devised the most beautiful means to clothe ourselves against our nakedness. At the end of our century, even these clothes are in tatters and through them we notice our nakedness again and we know suddenly we are primitive. *Electra* is the story of our primitive self and our primitive anger. It shows us that accepting our nakedness is the only way to an authentic future, the only chance for human beauty.

MG: I think the thing that haunted me most about *Electra* was the emphasis on vengeance. In the Judeo-Christian worldview, vengeance is not something we are taught to seek. Yet I can't help but wonder if there is something about the notion of vengeance that can speak to us today.

ZW: Vengeance could be called justice couldn't it? It brings to mind (former Chilean dictator Augusto) Pinochet who was arrested in London just six months ago for crimes against humanity. He's in his 80s. He's been going back and forth to England and they've been protecting him. And he's been responsible for the deaths of many thousand people. Do you then allow this man to carry on living in the lap of luxury while thousands of people have lost their brothers, sisters, uncles, aunts? Vengeance is not a nice thing. It doesn't get you anywhere. But we have to find some way to come to terms with our hatred or it will destroy us. In some ways, it has destroyed Electra.

MG: And, let's be honest, there is something very cleansing about vengeance.

ZW: Yes.

MG: When it is announced that "the deed is done" there is almost a sense of exhilaration.

ZW: Yes. The violence in *Electra* is the violence of the inconsolable heart. She is a woman for whom love is an absolute and beauty is a lost possession that is linked to the loss of her father. She is a heroine, a terrorist, and a meteoric soul. Her very contradictions are the source of her luminosity and fascination. I have not seen many Greek dramas, really, and now I am interested to see more. But it must connect with the audience. Unless it connects with an audience, I am not interested. Live performances should make you feel nourished in some way. I feel that unless you come out feeling nourished, there is no point. That is what we search for in the theater: we want to feel uplifted or challenged or fed.

MG: I recently read an interview with Brian Dennehy in which he spoke about his performance in *Death of a Salesman*. He said the hard part is not so much the physical strain—though his is also a very physical performance—

but the emotional strain. He said that it does deplete you in some way. How have you been affected by your performance in *Electra*?

ZW: Physically, what it did for me is I just fell apart after I finished the London run. Aches and pains and my back went out. Emotionally, you just have to do it. It is exhausting; however, I've learned that if I keep my physical stamina up, then my mental stamina just follows. Besides, your body will tell you when you've had enough. Ultimately, though, when David said "it's about time you had a good scream" he was absolutely right. My father died six years ago and my mother died four or five months before I started rehearsing for this play. So I had a lot to relate to and a lot of grief to give. There was definitely a sense of knowing what I was talking about.

MG: Is there a part of this experience that has helped you with your grief?

ZW: I don't know if it's helped. Perhaps it's helped. No, I don't think it has because, each night before the show, I play a mental videotape of the deaths of my parents. The days leading up to it. The moments before it. The days afterward. While that process has helped me prepare for my performance, I really don't need to go through that anymore. I don't *want* to go through that anymore. I don't want to go through that pain so much all the time. At a certain point, you have to stop. However, with a performance, you never use just one thing from your life, you use a lot of things. Not all of what I am feeling in *Electra* relates back to the death of my father. There are many other things going on. So, Brian's remark is absolutely right: you try not to take it home with you, you *can't* take it home with you, yet in some way it does stay in your psyche.

MG: How do you see this performance within the context of your career? Would you consider this your favorite role?

ZW: No, it's not my favorite. My favorite role was a non-speaking role: Kattrin in *Mother Courage*, which I did with Judi Dench at the Royal Shakespeare. The reason why it was my favorite was I didn't have any lines to learn and I died at the end and the audience was very sad! (Laughs) I say that flippantly, I don't really have favorite roles. When I am doing them, they are my favorite because you put your heart and soul into them. But, no, there are not favorite roles.

MG: This has been fascinating. Is there anything else you'd like to say about this adaptation of *Electra*?

ZW: The word passion comes to mind. Frank has a great mind. He was there for some rehearsals and his presence was exciting. On one hand you felt as though Sophocles was in the room and, on the other hand, it was as though we were working on a brand new play.